Taylor Swift

2   BACK TO DECEMBER

4   BLANK SPACE

6   FIFTEEN

8   I KNEW YOU WERE TROUBLE

10   LOVE STORY

12   MEAN

14   OUR SONG

16   PICTURE TO BURN

18   SHAKE IT OFF

20   SHOULD'VE SAID NO

22   TEARDROPS ON MY GUITAR

24   22

26   WE ARE NEVER EVER GETTING BACK TOGETHER

28   WHITE HORSE

30   YOU BELONG WITH ME

T0081924

To access audio visit:
www.halleonard.com/mylibrary

6232-1354-E260-6619

Audio Arrangements by Peter Deneff

ISBN 978-1-61780-571-4

HAL•LEONARD®
CORPORATION
7777 W. BLUEMOUND RD. P.O. BOX 13819 MILWAUKEE, WI 53213

Visit Hal Leonard Online at
www.halleonard.com

BACK TO DECEMBER

Words and Music by
TAYLOR SWIFT

Flute

BLANK SPACE

FLUTE

Words and Music by TAYLOR SWIFT,
MAX MARTIN and SHELLBACK

FIFTEEN

FLUTE

Words and Music by
TAYLOR SWIFT

I KNEW YOU WERE TROUBLE

FLUTE

Words and Music by TAYLOR SWIFT,
SHELLBACK and MAX MARTIN

LOVE STORY

FLUTE

Words and Music by
TAYLOR SWIFT

MEAN

FLUTE

Words and Music by
TAYLOR SWIFT

OUR SONG

FLUTE

Words and Music by
TAYLOR SWIFT

PICTURE TO BURN

FLUTE

Words and Music by TAYLOR SWIFT
and LIZ ROSE

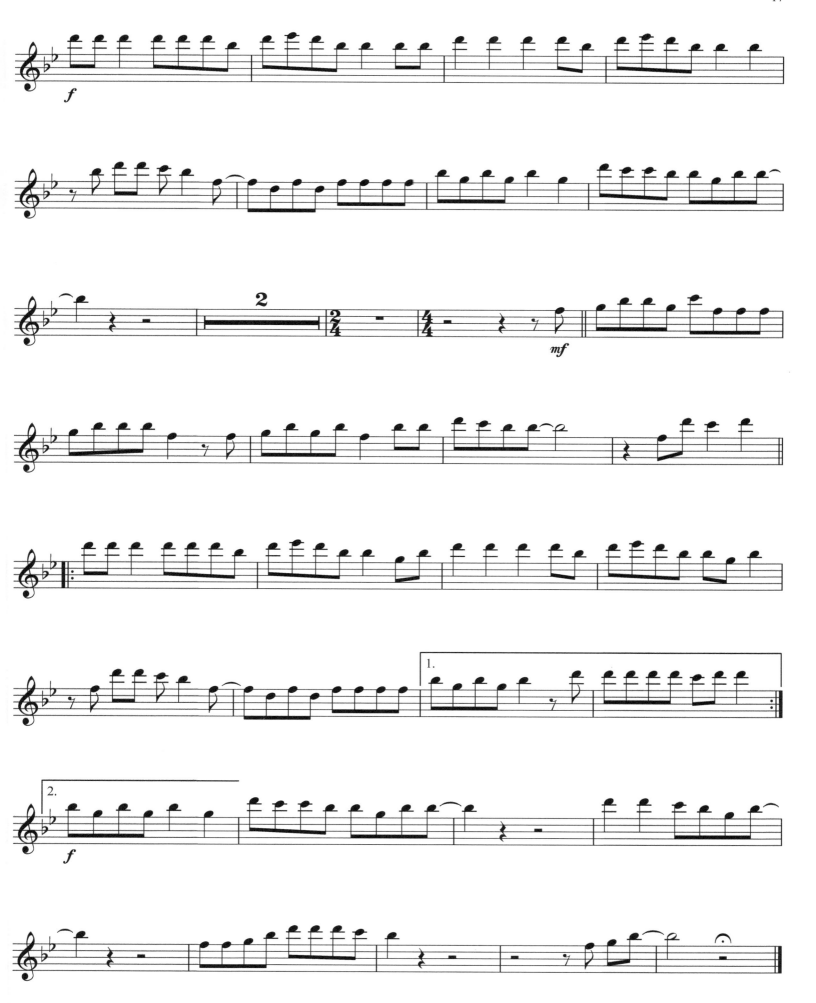

SHAKE IT OFF

FLUTE

Words and Music by TAYLOR SWIFT,
MAX MARTIN and SHELLBACK

SHOULD'VE SAID NO

FLUTE

Words and Music by
TAYLOR SWIFT

TEARDROPS ON MY GUITAR

Flute

Words and Music by TAYLOR SWIFT
and LIZ ROSE

23

22

FLUTE

Words and Music by TAYLOR SWIFT,
SHELLBACK and MAX MARTIN

WE ARE NEVER EVER GETTING BACK TOGETHER

FLUTE

Words and Music by TAYLOR SWIFT,
SHELLBACK and MAX MARTIN

WHITE HORSE

FLUTE

Words and Music by TAYLOR SWIFT
and LIZ ROSE

YOU BELONG WITH ME

FLUTE

Words and Music by TAYLOR SWIFT
and LIZ ROSE